The FAKE NEWS Crisis

How Misinformation Harms Society

Barbara Sheen

San Diego, CA

About the Author

Barbara Sheen is the author of 109 books for young people. She lives in New Mexico with her family. In her spare time she likes to swim, garden, walk, cook, and read.

Printed in the United States

For more information, contact:
ReferencePoint Press, Inc.
PO Box 27779
San Diego, CA 92198
www.ReferencePointPress.com

Picture Credits:
Cover: Ollyy/Shutterstock.com

6: lev radin/Shutterstock.com
10: BiksuTong/Shutterstock.com
12: Tom Williams/CQ Roll Call/Newscom
17: MAOIKO/Shutterstock.com
23: Paul Hennessy/Polaris/Newscom
26: Naresh777/Shutterstock.com
30: Ringo Chiu/Shutterstock.com
33: Fiora Watts/Shutterstock.com
41: Dustin Chamber/Reuters/Newscom
43: Aaron P Bernstein/Reuters/Newscom
46: Kaspars Grinvalds/Shutterstock.com
48: pcruciatti/Shutterstock.com

LIBRARY OF CONGRESS CATALOGING-IN-PUBLICATION DATA

Names: Sheen, Barbara, author.
Title: The fake news crisis : how misinformation harms society / Barbara Sheen.
Description: San Diego : ReferencePoint Press, 2021. | Includes bibliographical references and index.
Identifiers: LCCN 2021035619 (print) | LCCN 2021035620 (ebook) | ISBN 9781678202408 (library binding) | ISBN 9781678202415 (ebook)
Subjects: LCSH: Fake news--Juvenile literature. | Media literacy--Juvenile literature.
Classification: LCC PN4784.F27 S54 2021 (print) | LCC PN4784.F27 (ebook) | DDC 302.23--dc23
LC record available at https://lccn.loc.gov/2021035619
LC ebook record available at https://lccn.loc.gov/2021035620

CONTENTS

A Far-Reaching Problem

On January 6, 2021, the US Congress met in a joint session to formally certify the results of the 2020 presidential election. That same day, President Donald Trump held a political rally near the White House that was attended by thousands of his supporters. Since Election Day, Trump, who had lost the election, had been spreading the false narrative that the election was stolen from him due to widespread voter fraud. He made this claim even though it had been disproved. In fact, state and local judges, election officials, the Department of Justice, and the Department of Homeland Security all affirmed that Joe Biden had won fair and square. Nevertheless, Trump's allegations were amplified on social media and conservative broadcast news networks. By January 6, polls showed that about half of Republican voters accepted and trusted the president's claims. As St. Louis lawyer Albert Watkins explains, "The words . . . of a president are supposed to mean something."[1]

At the January 6 rally, Trump insisted that he had won the election and urged his supporters to fight to take back the country. Shortly thereafter, a crowd of more than eight hundred protesters marched to the Capitol in an attempt to overturn (what they were led to believe) was Biden's illegitimate victory. Things turned violent when the protesters stormed the building. They attacked and injured police officers, looted and vandalized government property, and threatened to execute Vice President Mike Pence and other lawmakers. In fear for their personal safety, the vice president, members of Congress, and their staffs were forced to flee or hide.

Long-Term Consequences

As a result of the insurrection, 5 people died, 140 people were injured, and more than 500 rioters were arrested. Yet in the months that followed, Trump continued pushing his false narrative. This fake news not only sowed doubt about the legitimacy of the 2020 election but also made many Americans lose trust in the entire electoral process. The Department of Homeland Security described the 2020 election as "the most secure in American history."[2] Even so, a June 2021 Monmouth University poll found that 69 percent of Republicans believed that voter fraud gave Biden the election victory. In the same poll, 29 percent said that they would never accept Biden as president.

Misinformation about the results of the election—and the distrust it fueled—has been divisive and harmful. As author Timothy Garton Ash explains, "To survive, democracy needs a minimum of shared truth. With the storming of the Capitol in Washington on 6 January, the US showed us just how dangerous it is when millions of citizens are led to deny an important, carefully verified fact."[3]

Making matters worse, the false narrative that led to the insurrection poses a long-term threat to the future of democratic elections in the United States. In

> "To survive, democracy needs a minimum of shared truth. With the storming of the Capitol in Washington on 6 January, the US showed us just how dangerous it is when millions of citizens are led to deny an important, carefully verified fact."[3]
>
> —Timothy Garton Ash, author

On January 6, 2021, responding to false claims that Donald Trump's electoral loss was the result of voter fraud, hundreds of protestors attacked the US Capitol in an attempt to disrupt congressional certification of the election.

response to Trump's allegations, counties in Arizona and Georgia ordered millions of ballots, which had already been recounted multiple times, to be recounted yet again. Other states may follow suit, despite the cost to taxpayers and the distrust it creates in the electoral process.

What is even more troubling is that as of May 2021, legislators in forty-eight states had proposed at least 389 bills that restrict voting access and would disproportionately affect minorities. These proposed laws seek to correct a problem that would indeed be serious if it were not the product of fake news. Allegations of voter fraud, which have yet to be supported by evidence, are rooted in fake news. In the process, these proposed laws are likely to increase racial tensions and political polarization in American society.

A Pervasive Problem

The fake news that led to the insurrection is part of a wider problem. Although some fake news stories are satirical and not intended to be taken seriously, others purposefully aim to do harm. Some stories circulate for only a short time, then fade away without causing much damage. Others persist, causing long-term harm. An article about a study linking childhood vaccines to autism appeared in the scientific journal the *Lancet* in 1998. Twelve years later, the *Lancet* retracted the article after the study was shown to be deeply flawed and the conclusion to be incorrect. The false claims linking vaccines and autism did not go away, however; they continue to circulate and influence people's actions today. Many wary parents have refused to vaccinate their children, leading to the resurgence of previously eliminated diseases and avoidable deaths.

Clearly, if it is left unchecked, fake news can have dangerous ramifications. It can undermine democracies, amplify racial tensions, and negatively impact public health. Fake news is a problem that affects everyone.

CHAPTER ONE

What Is Fake News?

In April 2021, US Olympic karate athlete Sakura Kokumai was exercising in a California park when a stranger threatened her. At first, Kokumai did not understand why she was being targeted; but when the man began spewing racial slurs, she realized she was the object of anti-Asian hate. "I was aware about the anti-Asian hate that was going on. You see it almost every day on the news," she said. "But I didn't think it would happen to me at a park I usually go to to train."[4]

Indeed, according to California State University's Center for the Study of Hate and Extremism, racist verbal and physical attacks on Asian Americans increased by an average of 150 percent in major US cities during the COVID-19 pandemic. Asian American rights groups attributed the increase to a widely circulated conspiracy theory alleging that the coronavirus was bioengineered in a Chinese laboratory and intentionally released. Some people who believed this claim retaliated by attacking Asian Americans.

False, Inaccurate, or Misleading

The conspiracy theory that led to the attack on Kokumai is a form of fake news. Fake news is false, inaccurate, or misleading information disguised as credible news. Unlike legitimate news, fake news is not checked for accuracy or credibility. Some fake news stories are easy to detect because they are silly and clearly not meant to be taken seriously. However, many fake news reports are difficult to distinguish from the truth. Rather than aiming to provide readers with an unbiased and true account of whatever is happening, these stories seek to spread distrust, manipulate public opinion, redirect blame, destroy reputations, or generate personal, political, or financial gain.

Some of these phony reports are totally fabricated. For instance, a March 2021 story claimed that the US Navy's special operations force had arrested former secretary of state Hillary Clinton for murder, child sex trafficking, and treason, among other crimes. According to the story, Clinton was taken to Guantánamo Bay, Cuba, where she was incarcerated, condemned by a military tribunal, and executed. In reality, none of these allegations was true. Yet the fabricated report gained so much traction that it was necessary for Clinton to appear on video to prove she had not been put to death. Nevertheless, her reputation was sullied and her safety was threatened by individuals who believed she had committed the crimes they had read about in the unsubstantiated story.

Other fake news stories have some basis in fact, but the facts are usually misrepresented to suit the writer's purpose. Leaving out important details, offering only one point of view, and/or using inflammatory language that evokes an emotional response from the reader are all tricks that creators of fake news employ. A recent story, which claimed that Biden was mentally unfit to be president, drew on misrepresented facts in an attempt to destroy his reputation. It employed inflammatory language, insinuating that Biden was unable to control his own faculties, much less run the country. The allegation, which had started circulating during the 2020 presidential campaign and continued to circulate in 2021, was based on the fact that Biden is sometimes hesitant in his speech. However, it ignored a very important detail: Biden has dealt with stuttering since childhood.

President Joe Biden addresses employees of the US Department of Defense. Fake news reports suggested that Biden's occasionally hesitant speech was the result of cognitive impairment. In reality, Biden has suffered from a speech impediment since childhood.

Despite the verifiable medical explanation for Biden's hesitant speech, once the story went viral, the damage was done. As author and Massachusetts Institute of Technology professor Sinan Aral explains,

> When fake news isn't completely fabricated, it typically distorts real-world information by tweaking or contorting it, mixing it with true information, and highlighting its most sensational and emotional elements. It then scales rapidly on social media and spreads faster than our ability to verify or debunk it. Once it spreads, it's hard to put back in the bottle and even harder to clean up, even with a healthy dose of the truth.[5]

Indeed, although this particular story did not tarnish Biden's reputation enough to derail his presidential campaign or force him out of office, it did reduce public confidence in his ability to serve. In fact, a February 2021 Insiders/Survey Monkey poll found that 33 percent of respondents believed Biden was mentally incompetent and, therefore, unfit to be president.

Different Categories of Fake News

The stories about Biden's mental competency are a type of fake news known as disinformation. The general term *fake news* is used to describe different types of untruths, including misinformation, disinformation, propaganda, and conspiracy theories. Misinformation is the least sinister. It is false information that is reported and spread without a deliberate intention to deceive. Anyone who has shared an inaccurate article that they believed to be true at the time is guilty of spreading misinformation. Disinformation, in contrast, is created and spread with the specific intent to deceive. So, if someone continues sharing an inaccurate article after learning it is false, he or she is spreading disinformation. According to the data-gathering company Statista, 10 percent of American adults knowingly share disinformation on social media.

"When fake news isn't completely fabricated, it typically distorts real-world information by tweaking or contorting it, mixing it with true information, and highlighting its most sensational and emotional elements."[5]

—Sinan Aral, author and Massachusetts Institute of Technology professor of management and data science

One blatant attempt to promote disinformation occurred in May 2021, when Congressman Andrew Clyde of Georgia likened the January 2021 insurrection at the Capitol to a normal tourist visit. During the insurrection, Clyde was photographed barricading the doors of the House Chamber to protect himself and other lawmakers from the rampaging crowd. Yet just a few months later, Clyde publicly denied he was ever in any danger.

Georgia congressman Andrew Clyde (second from top left) and security personnel use furniture to barricade an entrance to the House chamber in the US Capitol on January 6, 2021. Clyde later denied that the mob of protesters presented any danger to members of Congress.

Clyde's claim can also be classified as propaganda. Disinformation and misinformation that are aired for political purposes are propaganda, another type of fake news. Propaganda is usually created and circulated by governments and politicians to smear rival nations or political opponents, to distract people from real issues, or to promote a specific viewpoint or cause. Although most Americans associate propaganda with totalitarian regimes, all governments employ it. In the early twentieth century, President Theodore Roosevelt used propaganda in speeches and through staged photos to promote the construction of the Panama Canal. Years later, President Barack Obama used propaganda in speeches and on social media to gain support for the Affordable Care Act.

Conspiracy theories, another form of fake news, often contain a mixture of propaganda, misinformation, and disinformation. Conspiracy theories try to control or explain hard-to-understand events by blaming powerful people, institutions, businesses, or groups for whatever occurred. They often assert that important secrets are being withheld from the public. In addition, most conspiracy theories disregard rational thought. For instance, a 2020 conspiracy theory accused Wayfair, a popular online furniture retailer, of concealing missing children inside high-priced cabinets for the purpose of human trafficking. Other modern conspiracy theories are equally damaging to powerful institutions. They include the theory that President John F. Kennedy's assassination was masterminded by the Central Intelligence Agency, that recent school shootings were hoaxes staged by gun control advocates, and that a destructive 2021 Texas snowstorm was engineered by President Biden as an attack on Texas.

A Long History

Fake news, in all its forms, may seem like a modern invention. But it has actually been used for centuries to spread mistrust, manipulate the public, and gain profit. One example occurred more than two thousand years ago when the Roman politician Octavian sought to manipulate public opinion by sowing distrust about his political rival, Mark Antony. Octavian spread disinformation and propaganda claiming that Antony's loyalties lay with his lover, Cleopatra, the queen of Egypt, rather than with Rome and its citizens. Octavian's allegations helped him unseat Antony and become Rome's first emperor.

Centuries later, in 1835, in an attempt to boost its profits, a New York newspaper ran a series of articles claiming that a well-known astronomer had discovered life on the moon. The stories were quite detailed and included fictional illustrations of moon people. The scam worked. The series raised profits; however, it also caused some readers to panic, fearing that an invasion by moon people was coming. The publisher eventually admitted that the story was a hoax—but not until the newspaper had made significant financial gains.

In a more disturbing use of fake news, during the 1930s and 1940s, Adolf Hitler successfully spread disinformation and propaganda blaming a host of social issues on the Jewish people.

Hitler's goal was to manipulate the German public into supporting his anti-Semitic agenda. Ultimately, Hitler's unfounded claims led to many Germans supporting the slaying of an estimated 6 million Jews during the Holocaust.

More recently, former president Trump famously used misleading news to advance his political agenda. According to the *Washington Post*, Trump made more than thirty thousand false or misleading claims during his four years in office. Trump also repeatedly labeled verifiable news stories that did not promote his agenda as *fake news* as a way to discredit them. He then called his own fake stories corrections of the so-called fake news. Since many people did not know what to trust, this gambit gave actual fake news more traction. As former Federal Bureau of Investigation (FBI) deputy director Andrew McCabe writes in his book, *The Threat: How the FBI Protects America in the Age of Terror and Trump*, "A person such as the president can on impulse and with minimal effort inject any sort of falsehood into public conversation through digital media and call his own lie a correction of 'fake news.'"[6]

"A person such as the president can on impulse and with minimal effort inject any sort of falsehood into public conversation through digital media and call his own lie a correction of 'fake news.'"[6]

—Andrew McCabe, former deputy director of the FBI

How Does Fake News Spread?

In the twenty-first century, individuals use social media as a platform for circulating disinformation, something earlier creators and amplifiers of false information could not do. There is no doubt that the popularity of social media and other digital platforms has allowed untruths to spread faster and farther than ever before. Using social media, anyone—from a world leader to a teen—can freely view, generate, post, and spread fake news stories and

How Journalists Verify Information

Legitimate news organizations work hard to ensure that the information they deliver is true and accurate. Journalists employed by legitimate news organizations must thoroughly investigate a story before writing, posting, or broadcasting it. They interview witnesses and experts, search through official documents such as police reports, legal records, financial statements, and other reliable sources before preparing a draft of the story.

The draft is examined by a fact-checker. Fact-checkers use databases and reference books, among other resources, to verify that every statistic, name, and statement is accurate. Fact-checkers also flag anything in the article that could be misleading. Based on the fact-checker's input, the journalist prepares a final draft of the piece. It must be approved by an editor before it can be published, posted, or broadcast.

Despite these steps, errors occur. Once a story is published, posted, or aired, if a mistake is discovered, reputable news organizations publicly acknowledge and correct the error. In contrast, creators, posters, and spreaders of fake news rarely take these steps.

digitally altered photos. Such posts frequently go viral before they can be discredited. "It's as if, when you bought a book, they threw in the printing press for free; it's like you had a phone that could turn into a radio if you pressed the right buttons,"[7] says Clay Shirky, a professor of interactive telecommunications at New York University.

Social media is rife with trolls. These are people who post inflammatory messages, misinformation, and conspiracy theories online in hopes of provoking a response or manipulating attitudes. Often they seek to promote their own ideological beliefs, as well as to bully or damage the reputation of people or groups with whom they disagree. Trolls also attack verifiable news sources and other social media users whose ideas they oppose in order to discredit them. This strategy, according to David Lazer, a distinguished professor of political science and computer and information science at Northeastern University, "can enable discriminatory and inflammatory ideas to enter public discourse and be treated as fact. Once embedded, such ideas can in turn be used to create scapegoats, to normalize prejudices, to harden us-versus-them mentalities and even, in extreme cases, to catalyze and justify violence."[8]

Other fake news stories are spread rapidly by malicious bots, or robots using artificial intelligence (AI). AI is the science of using computer programs to simulate human intelligence. Programmers set up social media accounts for the bots so they appear to be real people. The bots then continuously post rumors, disinformation, and slanderous claims that manipulate public opinion. Some bots are programmed to interact with human visitors by replying to questions and comments about their posts, just as actual people do. This helps convince social media users that the bots are real people and the misinformation they spread is true.

Bots also helped to spread fake news for financial gain on websites and social media platforms through an advertising strategy known as clickbait. Clickbait consists of come-ons, which are designed to entice visitors to click on a link. Clicking on the link takes visitors to a web page where a related fake news article is located. Often, the web page itself is part of a fake news website that has been set up for the sole purpose of disseminating disinformation.

Host platforms receive a small fee every time someone clicks on one of these links, so they have a vested interest in users taking the bait. Therefore, the more visitors the host platform attracts, the greater the likelihood of people clicking on the bait and the more money the host platform earns. To attract more visitors and increase their earnings, social media platforms use algorithms to determine the news and clickbait that is delivered to a user's feed based on his or her interests. Although customizing information in this manner can enhance a user's experience on the platform, it also can be dangerous. A study published in the journal *Computers in Human Behavior* found that when people are exposed to information that supports their beliefs without

Many people now use cell phones to access news reports on social media, rather than traditional news sources. People can read and spread fake news using these sites.

being exposed to other points of view, they develop a distorted sense of reality. Consequently, they are more likely to accept false information as fact.

Lack of trust in traditional news sources, which has been amplified by politicians and trolls discrediting these sources, adds to the problem. According to Edelman, an international survey organization, more and more people have lost trust in traditional news sources. A 2021 survey found that between 2020 and 2021, trust in traditional media dropped by 8 percent. As a consequence, people are turning to social media for their news. In fact, a 2020

Fake News Websites

Fake news is often spread through fake news websites dedicated to producing and spreading misleading information and false claims. Although websites that publish satire usually post a small disclaimer alerting visitors that the material posted on the site is fictional, many visitors fail to read the disclaimer and accept the posts as fact. Nonsatirical fake news sites are less forthcoming. Their goal is to fool visitors, which they do in many ways.

In addition to spreading fake news via articles and stories, fake news websites often post digitally altered photos to promote a particular ideology. In fact, during the 2021 Black Lives Matter protests, a number of doctored photos were spread online in an effort to disparage the movement. For example, one altered photo made it look like Black Lives Matter protesters had brutally beaten a group of elderly white people, although this never occurred.

Doctored videos, known as deepfakes, are also becoming more common on fake news websites. These use AI to subtly alter voices and faces so that they are very difficult to distinguish from the real thing. Celebrities and politicians are often the victims of these videos, which seek to damage their reputations.

Pew Research Center survey found that 53 percent of Americans get their news from social media. Unfortunately, since clickbait, trolls, and bots thrive online, a large number of people are being fed a diet of lies that they believe to be true. "Social media are practically built for spreading fake news,"[9] says Norbert Schwarz, a psychologist who studies misinformation.

Why Do People Believe Fake News?

There are many reasons why people believe fake news. An old saying, which claims that people believe what they want to believe, seems to be true. Psychologists have found that people seek out and believe information that agrees with their personal beliefs and biases, as opposed to seeking out information that contradicts their worldview. Therefore, when social media users get news tailored to their interests, they are unlikely to seek out other accounts or attempt to fact-check the article's credibility. A

2018 study reported on the Social Science Research Network found that 56 percent of Facebook users could not identify false posts that aligned with their beliefs as fake news. In fact, individuals are apt to dismiss information that disagrees with their beliefs. And, according to other studies, the more extreme people's beliefs are, the more likely they are to accept false news that syncs with their beliefs.

Research also shows that people are more likely to accept misinformation as fact if it comes from someone they trust, such as a friend, family member, or public figure. A 2017 study conducted by the independent research organization NORC found that in determining the credibility of information, people focus more on the trustworthiness of the person sharing the information than on the original source of information. So, when people see something on social media posted by a friend, they generally view it in a positive way without questioning its veracity, irrespective of the original source. Plus, the greater the number of friends and other trusted sources posting this misinformation, and the more times this information is repeated, the more likely individuals will be influenced by and trust the material. "For the most part, our brains equate 'truth' with 'things we've seen said a lot by people we trust,'"[10] blogger and tech writer Mike Caulfield explains.

> "Social media are practically built for spreading fake news."[9]
>
> —Norbert Schwarz, psychologist

Regardless of the source of fake news, why it is shared, or why it is accepted as truth, the effect can be dangerous. For thousands of years, false information, in all its forms, has caused harm to society. Modern technology and the immense popularity of social media have amplified the problem, allowing fake news to spread faster and on a wider scale than ever before. "It's like a free-for-all," says Joan Donovan, the head of a Harvard University study of online disinformation. "It's almost unfathomable."[11]

Denying Science

Alex Jones is a popular radio host and conspiracy theorist who runs InfoWars, a far-right website. Throughout his career, Jones has used his InfoWars platform to spread anti-vaccination conspiracy theories. In 2020, Jones spread a conspiracy theory claiming that a secret cabal of powerful people, led by Microsoft founder Bill Gates, was plotting to depopulate and control Earth. To achieve their goal, they created and unleashed a bioengineered virus that caused COVID-19. They then funded the development of a vaccine implanted with chemicals and microchips designed to sicken, sterilize, kill, and/or damage the brains of those who received it. According to Jones, COVID-19 vaccines "destroy the immunity of some, give people autoimmune diseases . . . , and target the basic protein in the placenta so a woman will have miscarriages every time. . . . These vaccines don't protect you, they can kill you."[12]

Although there is no factual basis for these claims, they were widely promoted on InfoWars, social media, and conservative broadcast news outlets. In fact, just one video pushing this theory garnered at least 1.8 million views on YouTube and 1.2 million engagements on Facebook. A

2020 YouGov poll suggests that 28 percent of Americans believe the theory, with the percentage increasing to 48 percent among Republicans. Moreover, Americans were not the only ones taken in by these bogus claims. The theory spread so quickly on social media and was so widely accepted as true that an Italian lawmaker demanded that Gates be tried by the international court for crimes against humanity. Although Gates was never put on trial, his life was threatened repeatedly, and he was publicly labeled a mass murderer by Jones's followers.

What is even more troubling is that Jones's claims made many people hesitant to receive the COVID-19 vaccine, thereby prolonging the pandemic and endangering public health on a global scale. It also caused many people to lose trust in—and even threaten the lives of—lawmakers, health care professionals, public health officials, and scientists supporting vaccination.

QAnon

Followers of QAnon, an online conspiracy theory group, were among those who embraced and amplified Jones's theory. Like almost all conspiracy theories, Jones's theory contends that things are not what they seem. Most conspiracy theories blame powerful individuals for societal ills. They maintain that powerful people (who are also known as the "deep state") are trying to control the world by directing events, spreading misinformation, and covering up the truth. Although most conspiracy theories defy science and logic, they tap into people's need for answers and help believers make sense of challenging events such as the pandemic. As social scientist and author Jovan Byford explains, "Conspiracy theories flourish when social machinery breaks down and available ways of making sense of the world prove inadequate for what is going on."[13]

"Conspiracy theories flourish when social machinery breaks down and available ways of making sense of the world prove inadequate for what is going on."[13]

—Jovan Byford, social scientist

QAnon has its roots in a conspiracy theory claiming that a secret group, or cabal, of liberal politicians, celebrities, and other powerful people run a global child sex trafficking ring. Group members, the conspiracy charges, molest, kill, and perform satanic, cannibalistic rituals on captive children. The theory also alleges that members of the group control the media, governments, and financial institutions worldwide. These powerful people, according to the theory, have been working to discredit Trump, who, conspiracy theorists say, is trying to dismantle the cabal. As far-fetched as this theory sounds, a March 2021 poll conducted by the Public Religion Research Institute found that one in five—or about 11 million—Republicans believe the theory. Moreover, many QAnon adherents believe that to destroy the cabal and thereby end the attack on children, Trump must be reinstated as president, even if doing so involves violence.

QAnon's conspiracy theories are posted on the internet as cryptic puzzles and riddles by an anonymous source known as Q, who claims to have high national security clearance. Special apps alert followers to the posts. Followers share and circulate the posts on social media as they try to make sense of the mysterious messages. Since Q's first posts in October 2017, the movement's popularity has grown throughout the world. As QAnon grew, group leaders and members spread a large range of other conspiracy theories. Some of these theories used the child sex trafficking theory as the foundation for other theories related to the COVID-19 pandemic. One of these alleged that the coronavirus that causes COVID-19 was bioengineered and released by members of the child trafficking cabal to bring down Trump, thereby keeping him from ending their evil operation. Another claimed that mask-wearing regulations endanger children. The theory maintained that masking children makes it difficult for them to cry for help if they are snatched by sex traffickers. Therefore, in a misguided effort to protect young family members, many QAnon adherents refused to let their children wear masks even though masking is a proven way to mitigate the spread of the virus.

Followers of the conspiracy theory group known as QAnon attend a Trump rally in 2018. QAnon followers claim that Trump must be reinstated as president in order to dismantle a secret cabal of child sex traffickers, among other unfounded beliefs.

Other QAnon theories related to the pandemic are not linked to the sex trafficking theory, but they still place blame on powerful groups and individuals. For example, many QAnon followers insist that telecommunication companies used radio waves emanating from 5G mobile phone towers to spread COVID-19. This notion led to a rash of attacks on 5G towers and telecommunication workers in Europe. Great Britain reported fifty fires targeting towers and 5G equipment in April 2020 alone. Multiple attacks on 5G towers were also reported in Belgium, Cyprus, Ireland, and the Netherlands.

These 5G towers relay data between wireless devices quickly and easily. Thus, attacks on the towers were especially distressing during the pandemic, when field hospitals depended on wireless service to communicate with medical suppliers, laboratories, and traditional hospitals. Likewise, quarantined patients and their families relied on smartphones and tablets to communicate with one another. As Nick Jeffery, the chief executive officer of the wireless carrier Vodafone UK, explained in 2020, "It's heart-rending enough that families cannot be there at the bedside of loved ones who are critically ill. It's even more upsetting that even the small solace of a phone or video call may now be denied them because of the selfish actions of a few deluded conspiracy theorists."[14]

"It's heart-rending enough that families cannot be there at the bedside of loved ones who are critically ill. It's even more upsetting that even the small solace of a phone or video call may now be denied them because of the selfish actions of a few deluded conspiracy theorists."[14]

—Nick Jeffery, chief executive officer of the wireless carrier Vodafone UK

A "Disinfodemic"

The popularity and influence of QAnon's theories grew during the COVID-19 pandemic, as did other conspiracy theories spread by individuals, groups, and some high-ranking government officials. Indeed, as the pandemic increased around the globe, so did a pandemic of misinformation, which researchers named a "disinfodemic." "There seems to be barely an area left untouched by disinformation in relation to the COVID-19 crisis," says Guy Berger, the director for policies and strategies regarding communication and information at the United Nations Educational Scientific and Cultural Organization, explains. "The big risk is that any single falsehood that gains traction can negate the significance of a body of true facts. When disinformation is repeated and amplified, including by influential people, the grave danger is that information which is based on truth, ends up having only marginal impact."[15]

Stuck at home, people spent a great deal of time on social media and fake news websites searching for easy answers. Conspiracy theories disputing the seriousness of the virus and the need for wearing a mask, social distancing, and lockdowns and promoting phony treatments and cures provided many of these answers. Despite scientific evidence to the contrary, millions of individuals adopted these false notions, putting public health at risk.

Some of the most dangerous theories disparaged real news concerning the seriousness of COVID-19, insisting the illness was no more serious than the flu. Theories that the pandemic was a hoax and that verifiable news reports of overcrowded hospitals and soaring death rates were lies spread almost as fast as the virus. In April 2020 alone, the Corona Virus Fact Alliance, a group of more than one hundred fact-checkers who publish and share information related to COVID-19, recorded nearly four thousand coronavirus-related hoaxes circulating around the world.

The United Nations Battles Conspiracy Theories

Americans are not the only people threatened by conspiracy theories that deny and delegitimize science. Conspiracy theories related to the COVID-19 pandemic so endangered public health on a global scale that the United Nations (UN) got involved in battling these theories. In 2020 the UN launched Verified, an online initiative to spread and amplify scientific information about COVID-19. As part of the initiative, local people in countries throughout the world signed up to be information volunteers. These volunteers receive a daily news feed with facts about the pandemic, which counter misinformation and conspiracy theories. Volunteers share this verified information with members of their community. Information volunteers include members of various UN agencies, business and media organizations, celebrities and media influencers, and teams of health care professionals.

Similarly, the World Health Organization (WHO), the agency that led the UN's response to the pandemic, added a "Mythbuster" page to its online coronavirus advice page. The page, according to an article on the UN News website, "refutes a staggering array of myths, including claims that drinking potent alcoholic drinks, exposure to high temperatures, or conversely, cold weather, can kill the virus." Colorful graphics and simple explanations helped make the page appealing to people of all ages and education levels.

United Nations, "During This Coronavirus Pandemic, 'Fake News' Is Putting Lives at Risk: UNESCO," UN News, April 2020. https://news.un.org.

To prove claims that the pandemic was a hoax, influential conspiracy theory supporters urged their followers to sneak into hospitals and take photos of empty waiting rooms, corridors, beds, and intensive care units—and then post these pictures on social media. QAnon also created the hashtag *#filmyourhospital* to encourage its followers to participate.

As a result, images depicting deserted hospital waiting rooms flooded social media. One YouTube video was viewed 270,000 times. Nevertheless, the theory was false. The pandemic was not a hoax. While it raged, hospital waiting rooms were purposefully kept empty to reduce the risk of transmission. For the same reason, COVID-19 patients were kept isolated, and visitors were not allowed into patients' rooms. Nevertheless, fake news denying the seriousness or the very existence of COVID-19 helped fuel the pandemic. It led many people to conclude that there was no

President Trump spread a false and dangerous theory that ingesting or injecting household cleaners could cure COVID-19.

reason to observe safety regulations. As a result, many of these individuals were angry when these regulations were enforced. In fact, it helped prompt anti-lockdown protests across the world, some of which turned violent, causing injuries to police officers and demonstrators and damage to public and private property. It also inspired a misguided group's attempt to kidnap Michigan governor Gretchen Whitmer in protest of what it viewed as the unnecessary safety regulations her administration imposed.

Members of the Trump administration helped to amplify these theories. Trump personally spread a dangerous theory concerning bogus prevention and cures. During a press briefing in April 2020, he suggested that ingesting or injecting household disinfectants could cure the virus. In reality, most household cleansers are poisonous. Taking them internally can cause fatal liver, respiratory, and heart failure. Scientists, health care professionals, and the makers of Lysol warned of the danger, and Trump later said he had been joking. Nevertheless, his claim took off on social media. In fact, it seems to have influenced some people to act recklessly. According to the American Association of Poison Control Centers, deaths from poisoning due to household disinfectants rose significantly in the weeks after Trump's remarks.

Anti-mask Conspiracies

Conspiracy theories about mask wearing also abounded. Almost all claimed that wearing a mask does not protect people from getting or transmitting COVID-19. Numerous studies disputed this claim. Research shows that the coronavirus spreads through the air on tiny respiratory droplets when infected people cough, sneeze, or speak. Wearing a mask helps guard people from spreading or being infected with these droplets.

Dozens of other fanciful anti-mask conspiracy theories circulated throughout the pandemic. They included claims that masking mandates were part of a plan by the so-called deep state to train the public to obey authority and allegations that wearing a mask causes the wearer to get carbon dioxide poisoning. Many

COVID-19 Vaccine Conspiracy Theories Threaten Some Educators' Jobs

Conspiracy theories related to COVID-19 vaccines could cause some Florida educators to lose their jobs. In April 2021, leaders of the Centner Academy, a private school located in Miami, warned teachers that the school would not employ vaccinated educators. "We cannot allow recently vaccinated people to be near our students until more information is known. . . . Reports have surfaced recently of non-vaccinated people being negatively impacted by interacting with people who have been vaccinated," the school's cofounder and longtime anti-vaxxer Leila Centner wrote in a letter to teachers. In the letter, she alluded to an unfounded conspiracy theory that unvaccinated females have experienced infertility, miscarriages, menstrual problems, and other reproductive issues through contact with vaccinated people, who, according to Centner, "may be transmitting something."

In reality, this is biologically impossible. The school's policy alarmed public health officials. However, as a private business, the school has the right to enforce its policy, forcing some educators to choose between their health and their livelihood—or, more broadly, between science and fake news.

Katie Shepherd, "Florida School Tells Teachers to Skip Vaccine," *Las Cruces (NM) Sun News*, April 28, 2021, p. A9.

people accepted this misinformation over scientific fact and refused to mask up. Their actions not only made them open to infection but also helped spread the virus, causing avoidable deaths. A June 2020 Virginia Commonwealth University study compared COVID-19 deaths across 198 countries to assess the impact of masking in public. Researchers found that, per capita, deaths increased an average of 8 percent per week in countries where the public favored mask wearing as compared with 54 percent per week in countries where the public was reluctant to wear masks.

Vaccine Hesitancy

The belief in conspiracy theories related to COVID-19 not only affected public health but also resulted in attacks and threats on the character and competence of public health officials and medical scientists who tried to counter the barrage of false information with scientific evidence. In fact, some public health officials' lives were threatened. Worse yet, it led to an attack on science itself. "We are facing a dangerous barrage of misinformation that ignores evidence and dismisses the scientific process, undermining our national response and belief in science,"[16] Dr. Ashish Jha, dean of the Brown University School of Public Health, said in 2020.

It caused so much distrust of logic and science that even after safe and effective vaccines became available, large numbers of people refused to be vaccinated. A 2021 National Public Radio poll found that one in four Americans said they would refuse to get a COVID-19 vaccine. Similar attitudes were revealed in polling done in other countries. A 2020 Gallup poll, for instance, found that nearly three in ten—or 1.3 billion—adults worldwide were unwilling to be vaccinated. In many cases, refusal was based on anti-vaccination conspiracy theories claiming that the vaccine posed greater danger than COVID-19. One theory maintained that the vaccine altered human DNA, changing the gender or sexuality of children. Another claimed that the vaccine was less effective in protecting against COVID-19 than the body's immune system. Still another alleged that the vaccine contained microchips that the government used to control and track people. The wildest theories falsely claimed that adverse reactions to the vaccine caused more American deaths than the virus itself. By denying science, these theories harm believers as well as nonbelievers.

> "We are facing a dangerous barrage of misinformation that ignores evidence and dismisses the scientific process, undermining our national response and belief in science."[16]
>
> —Dr. Ashish Jha, dean of the Brown University School of Public Health

Many unvaccinated individuals will sicken and die unnecessarily. Moreover, as the virus circulates among them, it is likely to mutate, forming new variants that may be more lethal than the

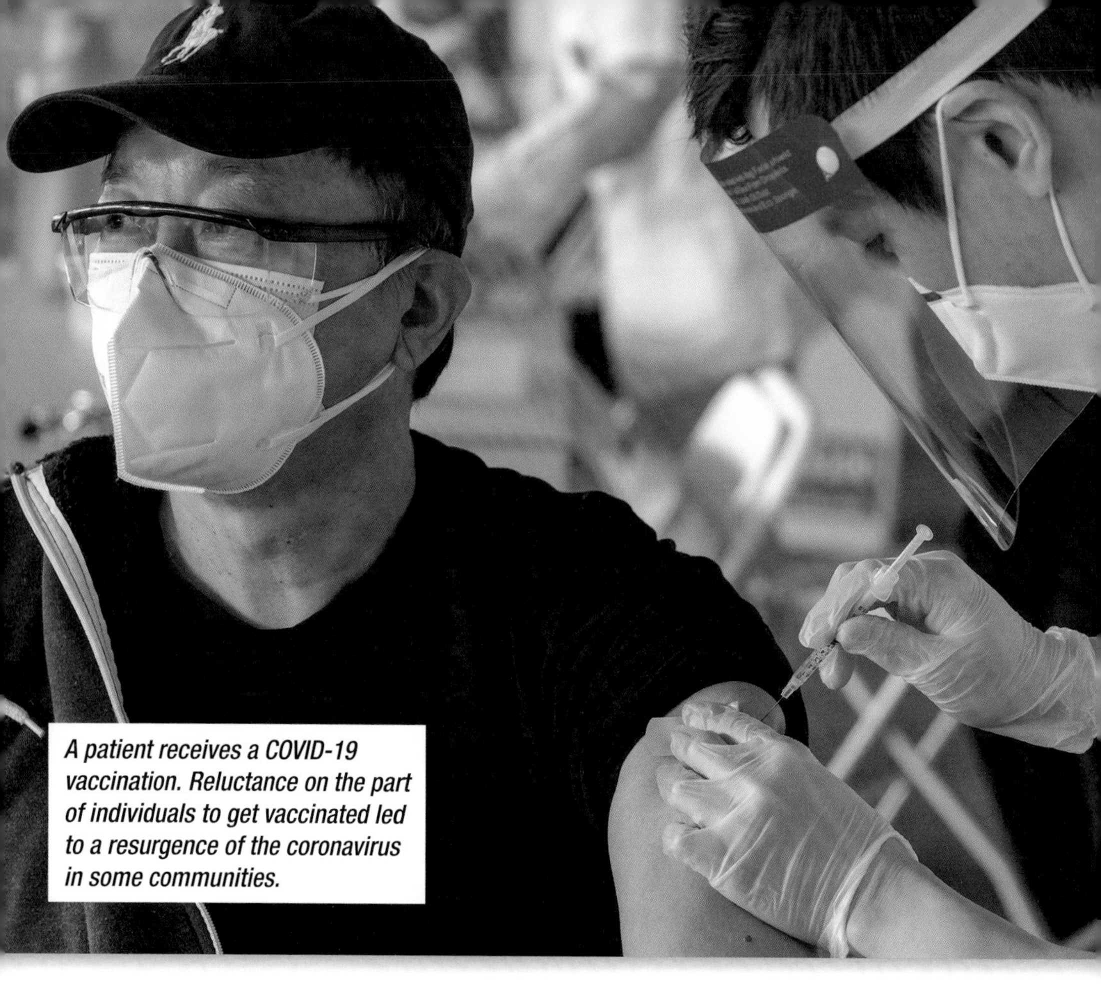

A patient receives a COVID-19 vaccination. Reluctance on the part of individuals to get vaccinated led to a resurgence of the coronavirus in some communities.

original virus. One of these, known as the Delta variant, began circulating in the United States during the summer of 2021. More contagious than the original virus, it spread rapidly among unvaccinated individuals. By mid-July 2021, new cases of COVID-19 had fallen dramatically in communities with high vaccination rates. In contrast, infections and hospitalizations increased in vulnerable communities where vaccination rates were low. According to the Centers for Disease Control and Prevention (CDC), 83 percent of these new cases were traced to the Delta variant.

In Alabama, for example, where only about one-third of the population is vaccinated, hospitalizations from COVID-19 more than doubled in one week in mid-July 2021. Mississippi, which has one of the lowest vaccine rates in the country, reported more than twenty-three hundred new cases between July 16 and July

19. This was the state's largest three-day increase in cases since February 2021. Other states with low vaccination rates, such as Arkansas, Florida, Kansas, Louisiana, and Missouri, among others, also experienced a large increase in new cases. And, as the virus continues to circulate, even more unvaccinated individuals are likely to fall ill. Some of these individuals will suffer long-term health issues linked to the coronavirus, which require ongoing care. As a result, insurance premiums and health care costs could soar in the future, costing the government and taxpayers millions of dollars. In an interview with the Cable News Network (CNN), US Surgeon General Vivek Murthy had this to say: "I am worried about what is to come because we are seeing increasing cases among the unvaccinated in particular. And while, if you are vaccinated, you are very well protected against hospitalization and death, unfortunately that is not true if you're unvaccinated."[17]

Dangerous Denial

It is dangerous to believe in unproven conspiracy theories and misinformation that denies science. False narratives were instrumental in raising fear and mistrust about pandemic-related issues. They helped facilitate the original spread of the virus. And, despite the availability of effective vaccines, false claims that question the safety of the vaccine are likely to help keep the pandemic going. According to most experts, only high levels of vaccination will prevent future outbreaks. As Dr. Walter Orenstein, the associate director of the Emory Vaccine Center and the former director of the CDC's immunization program, told public health officials in 2021, "This virus will not eradicate itself."[18]

Stoking Divisiveness

George Floyd was an African American man who was killed during his arrest in May 2020 by Derek Chauvin, a Minneapolis police officer. Chauvin pressed his knee into Floyd's neck, causing Floyd to suffocate as three other police officers looked on. In response to Chauvin's death, protesters took to the streets of Minneapolis in support of the Black Lives Matter movement, a political and social movement championing racial equality and police reform. The protests quickly spread throughout the world and continued during the summer. A 2020 Civis Analytics poll estimated that 15 to 26 million people participated in the protests in the United States.

The protests were largely peaceful; however, looting, arson, and vandalism occurred in some cities. In separate testimony before Congress in 2020, both FBI director Christopher Wray and former attorney general William Barr reported that trolls associated with the Russian, Chinese, and Iranian governments had exploited the demonstrations, flooding social media with misinformation and propaganda related to the protests, Floyd's death, and racial injustice in America. The goal was to weaken the

United States by fomenting distrust, divisiveness, and violence between supporters and opponents of the Black Lives Matter movement. According to a review by Politico of social media activity between May 30 and June 1, 2020, Russian and Chinese agents tweeted more than twelve hundred times about racial unrest and violence in the United States, using hashtags like *#BlackLivesMatter*.

In an effort to widen the gulf between Black Lives Matters activists and opponents, these posts depicted the protests as being far more violent and destructive than they actually were. Many of these posts portrayed the United States as being on the brink of collapse. They equated social issues leading up to the protests to the failure of democracy as a form of government. In contrast, they depicted their own authoritarian governments as peaceful, utopian alternatives. These actions not only added to discord in the United States but also damaged the way the United States was viewed by people in other nations.

Marchers demand justice in relation to George Floyd's murder following his arrest, during which he was kneeled on by a Minneapolis police officer. The officer was later convicted of murdering Floyd.

When asked about China's response to the protests, State Department spokesperson Morgan Ortagus had this to say: "We know that they are trying to take this opportunity to make comparisons to try to sow discord in the U.S. . . . We've seen a convergence between China, Russia and Iran spreading each other's disinformation on Twitter, on Facebook, the internet."[19]

"We've seen a convergence between China, Russia and Iran spreading each other's disinformation on Twitter, on Facebook, the internet."[19]

—Morgan Ortagus, US State Department spokesperson

Playing Politics

Spreading fake news related to American elections and politics is another way that foreign agents try to sow discord and divisiveness in the United States and strengthen their own agenda. For example, according to US intelligence agencies, Russian agents, bots, and trolls planted and spread disinformation across social media to influence the 2016 presidential election on Trump's behalf. In these posts, they smeared Democratic presidential nominee Hillary Clinton, accusing her of everything from murder to selling weapons to terrorist organizations. At the same time, they praised Trump, whose policies appeared to be more favorable to Russia than Clinton's.

Twitter reported that in the months leading up to the 2016 election, trolls working for Russia's Internet Research Agency posted an estimated 10 million tweets related to the election from four thousand fake accounts, many of which masqueraded as mainstream news organizations. They were also responsible for at least one thousand YouTube videos and, according to Facebook, hundreds of thousands of Instagram posts. Russian bots massively retweeted these posts, which were read and shared by millions of Americans who were unaware of the source.

In 2017 the Department of Justice launched an investigation into Russia's involvement in the election, which was led by former FBI director Robert Mueller. Mueller concluded that Russian agents conspired to sway the election in favor of Trump. Speaking at a 2017 press conference about Russia's misinformation campaign, Senator Mark Warner of Virginia, the highest-ranking Democrat on the Senate Intelligence Committee, said,

> What really concerns me [are reports] there were upwards of 1,000 paid internet trolls working out of a facility in Russia. . . .
>
> An outside foreign adversary effectively sought to hijack the most critical democratic process, the election of a president, and in that process, decided to favor one candidate over another.[20]

Spreading Misinformation in Europe

Fake news is a global problem. Extremist groups in Europe are known to use social media to affect politics, manipulate public opinion, and influence elections. In 2019, for instance, the European Union (EU) held an election for the European Parliament, a legislative group that governs the EU. Independent investigators hired by Avaaz, an online activist group, found that a network of far-right Facebook accounts linked up with each other to influence the elections. Facebook managed to remove some of these accounts before the election began. Even so, their messages were viewed more than a half billion times.

As part of their message, these groups spread hate. According to an article in *The Guardian*, Avaaz

> reported more than 500 suspect groups and Facebook pages operating across France, Germany, Italy, the [United Kingdom], Poland and Spain. Most were either spreading fake news or using false pages and profiles to artificially boost the content of parties or sites they supported, in violation of Facebook's rules. . . . Activity ranged from French accounts sharing white supremacist content, to posts in Germany supporting Holocaust denial. . . . In Italy, tactics included setting up general interest pages . . . then after followers signed up, transforming them into political tools.

Emma Graham-Harrison, "Far-Right Facebook Groups 'Spreading Hate to Millions in Europe,'" *The Guardian*, May 22, 2019. www.theguardian.com.

Beyond 2016

The impact of Russia's fake news campaign on Trump's 2016 victory was one of the most contested controversies of his presidency. Yet foreign meddling in American politics did not end with the 2016 election. Fearful that foreign agents would once again interfere in the 2020 election, social media companies shut down a network of suspicious Russian accounts. But this did not stop America's adversaries from launching a disinformation campaign to influence the outcome of the 2020 election. A 2021 report issued by the Office of the Director of National Intelligence (ODNI) found that Russia, Iran, Cuba, Venezuela, and Lebanon's militant Hezbollah group all tried to influence the election. Once again, Russian trolls posted misinformation on social media supporting Trump's reelection and discrediting his opponent, Biden. At the same time, they enlarged on unproven allegations made by Trump that if he lost the election, it would be due to voter fraud. The latter was part of Russia's ongoing goal of weakening the United States by undermining Americans' confidence in the electoral process.

Russian posts earned thousands of shares across social media, exacerbating discord and divisiveness among Americans. Russian agents also fed misinformation to right-wing media outlets and Trump's associates. The ODNI surmised that the Russians expected these outlets and individuals would spread the misinformation and also channel it to Trump to use for his own advantage. In fact, in 2020, Trump was warned by the FBI and by former National Security adviser Robert O'Brien that Rudy Giuliani, Trump's personal attorney, was the target of a Russian campaign to direct misinformation to Trump. As the ODNI report states, "A key element of Moscow's strategy this election cycle was its use of proxies linked to Russian intelligence to push influence narratives—including misleading or unsubstantiated allegations against President Biden—to US media organizations, US officials, and prominent US individuals, including some close to former President Trump and his administration."[21]

Elizabeth Cheney vs. Misinformation

Wyoming congresswoman Elizabeth Cheney is a conservative Republican. As the Republican House Conference chair, she was the third-highest-ranking Republican in the House of Representatives. Although Cheney has an excellent record of supporting conservative legislation, in May 2021 she was ousted from her high-ranking position by Trump loyalists in Congress. Her removal came about because she refused to support the misinformation that the election was stolen from Trump due to election fraud. She repeatedly and forcefully spoke out against this phony allegation. She maintained that anyone who tried to convince the American public that the election was invalid was guilty of spreading a dangerous lie that could undermine the democratic process. "The 2020 presidential election was not stolen," Cheney said in a tweet. "Anyone who claims it was is spreading THE BIG LIE, turning their back on the rule of law, and poisoning our democratic system."

She also repeatedly warned about the danger of politicians spreading stories that downplayed the seriousness of the January 6 attack on the Capitol. In an interview with CNN, Cheney said, "We can't whitewash what happened on January 6. . . . It is a threat to democracy." Despite the consequences, Cheney refused to embrace and spread fake news for political gain. Instead, she chose to defend real facts and the Constitution.

Allan Smith et al., "Cheney Hits Back at Trump over Election 'Big Lie,'" Yahoo! News, May 4, 2021. https://news.yahoo.com.

Iran, on the other hand, used social media to spread misinformation undercutting Trump's reelection efforts. According to the ODNI report, Iran "carried out a multi-pronged covert influence campaign intended to undercut former President Trump's reelection prospects—though without directly promoting his rivals—undermine public confidence in the electoral process and US institutions, and sow division and exacerbate societal tensions in the US."[22]

Domestic Extremists Spread Fake News

Foreign agents are not the only ones spreading lies that advance their own agenda while inflaming and dividing Americans. Members of domestic extremist groups also pose a significant threat. Trolls connected to these groups are skilled at spreading misinformation and conspiracy theories that discredit their political enemies while promoting hostility and violence.

In the run-up to the 2020 presidential election, right-wing extremist groups set up fake news websites, fake social media accounts, and private Facebook groups to spread misinformation that glorified Trump and defamed his political opponents. Trump and those close to him took this misinformation and enlarged on it, making it seem like real news, which extremist groups embraced and recirculated. "The disinformation spread by Donald Trump doesn't typically start with him," explains Graham Brookie, director of the Atlantic Council's Digital Forensic Research Lab, a bipartisan think tank in Washington, DC. "It is the endpoint in a supply chain of disinformation—the tip of an iceberg with an ecosystem of right-wing media, influencers, and outright conspiracy theorists making up the bulk below."[23]

Indeed, even before Election Day, extremist groups advanced Trump's false narrative that if he did not win, it would be because the election was rigged. In many of their posts, group members encouraged armed violence as a way to "stop the steal." In the days leading up to the January 6 insurrection, forum boards on websites popular with extremist groups accused prominent Democrats and election officials of treason.

Once Biden won the election, extremist groups continued to spread misinformation and conspiracy theories perpetuating the falsehood that the election was stolen from Trump. Inspired by these claims, Brian Maiorana, a white nationalist, threatened to retaliate against those he believed were instrumental in the fraud. Via social media, he threatened to kill Democrats, specific politicians, and destroy federal buildings, and he called for other extremists to join him. In his posts, he called for the "extermination of anyone that claims to be Democrat . . . as well as their family members."[24] In another post, he advocated bombing FBI headquarters.

Maiorana was arrested by the FBI before he could make good on his threats. But he was not alone in embracing fake news and advocating for violence. Other extremist group members were instrumental in promoting and participating in the January 6 insurrection. Even after Biden took office, extremists continued to keep alive the groundless assertion that Trump was the rightful president. They also added a new conspiracy theory that Trump would be reinstated as president in June 2021. When that did not happen, the date was changed to August 2021. In reality, there is no constitutional way for this to occur. Therefore, some of the posts suggested starting a civil war to achieve Trump's reinstatement. A February 2021 military coup d'etat in Myanmar that was provoked by allegations of election fraud in that nation was used as an example. As *Washington Post* columnist Philip Bump explains, "It's hard to overstate how damaging this claim [of US election fraud] has been . . . how far the tendrils of these claims about rampant voter fraud reach. . . . It's a hydra of misinformation in which slicing off one false claim simply spurs Trump's base to elevate a dozen more."[25]

"It's hard to overstate how damaging this claim has been . . . how far the tendrils of these claims about rampant voter fraud reach. . . . It's a hydra of misinformation in which slicing off one false claim simply spurs Trump's base to elevate a dozen more."[25]

—Philip Bump, journalist

Unethical Political Leaders

In an effort to remain in power, Trump and his political allies spread fake news that fueled foreign adversaries and domestic extremist groups and hurt the United States. The misinformation they disseminated increased the schism between Democrats and Republicans and caused many Americans to doubt the legitimacy of democratic practices, election officials, and government institutions. Unfortunately, although political leaders are supposed to put the needs of their constituents first, some spread false information in an effort to strengthen their own agenda, despite the consequences. For example, according to Vice News, at least nineteen state Republican Party chairpersons cast doubts on the validity of the 2020 election. Kelli Ward, the Arizona Republican Party chairwoman, even claimed that Biden's win was an illegal seizure of the government. Other Republican lawmakers downplayed the seriousness of the January 6 insurrection to curry favor among right-wing extremists. Some, such as Congresswoman Jody Hice of Georgia, went as far as to push the false narrative that the rioters were innocent victims. Despite the death of a Capitol police officer and injuries to others, Hice claimed that "it was Trump supporters who lost their lives that day, not Trump supporters who were taking the lives of others."[26]

Hice's claim was based on the fact that the deaths of four civilians were connected to the insurrection. Of these fatalities, two died of natural causes, one of a drug overdose. The fourth, Ashli Babbitt, was fatally shot by a US Capitol police officer as she tried to crawl through a barricaded door into an area of the House Chamber where lawmakers were sheltering from the angry mob. Congressman Ruben Gallegos of Arizona was in the House Chamber at the time. He maintained that the Capitol police risked their own lives to protect the legislators.

Indeed, even though the officer who shot Babbitt was investigated and cleared of any wrongdoing, another politician, Congressman Paul Gosar of Arizona, intensified Hice's claims. Taking his cue from misinformation posted on far-right message boards, Gosar asserted that Babbitt was a martyr who was executed by the officer who, he insisted, was lying in wait for a victim. Muddying the waters even further, Russian president Vladimir Putin used Hice's and Gosar's claims as a source of propaganda. He argued that Babbitt's shooting was proof that the United States stifles dissent and targets it citizens for their political beliefs, just as Russia is accused of doing.

Congresswoman Marjorie Taylor Greene of Georgia and Congressman Matt Gaetz of Florida were also involved in circulating false information concerning the insurrection. They helped

Representatives Matt Gaetz and Marjorie Taylor Greene have helped spread the conspiracy theory that the mob that attacked the US Capitol on January 6, 2021, actually consisted of FBI agents masquerading as Trump supporters.

spread the conspiracy theory that the mob that ransacked the Capitol was actually FBI agents masquerading as Trump supporters. Greene, who has repeatedly endorsed QAnon conspiracy theories, also spread the unsubstantiated claim that the people who were arrested for participating in the insurrection were being held under harsh conditions such as solitary confinement. She also circulated divisive claims about other issues. She compared COVID-19 precautions such as mask wearing and vaccine requirements to the Holocaust, likened Democrats and vaccine workers to Nazis, and spread misinformation maligning Anthony Fauci, President Biden's chief medical adviser during the pandemic, among other allegations.

Other phony stories pushed by politicians are less destructive but are still damaging. One example is a 2021 story that was promoted by Donald Trump Jr., Congresswoman Lauren Boebert of Colorado, and Texas governor Greg Abbott and was amplified on social media and right-wing broadcast networks. It alleged that, as part of President Biden's plan to reduce greenhouse gases associated with animal agricultural emissions, he planned to limit how much meat Americans could consume. Although entirely untrue, the story raised deep concerns among members of the meat industry and widened the divide between people who support environmental regulations and those who do not.

Democrats Are Not Blameless

Even though many recent fake news posts, such as the meat-rationing story, can be attributed to conservative politicians, Democrats are not blameless. They spread misinformation too. During the 2020 presidential campaign, Biden made a number of false claims in an effort to manipulate public opinion and gain support for his candidacy. For example, in April 2019, Biden claimed that the 2017 Tax Cuts and Jobs Act, which was signed into law by Trump, only gave tax cuts to corporations and high-income earners. This is untrue. Although the tax cuts did benefit the wealthy and corporations, they also benefited regular people. The nonpartisan Tax Policy Center reports that 65 percent of households paid less taxes in 2018 than in 2017 under the act.

Once he took office, Biden added to this false narrative. He said that the tax cuts had not improved economic growth and that the Heritage Foundation, a conservative think tank, agreed with his assessment. In reality, the Heritage Foundation maintained that the tax cuts were working. Although these false claims did not cause serious damage, they furthered the divide and lack of trust between Democrats and Republicans on tax issues.

Other prominent Democrats have circulated misinformation about their political opponents. For instance, in 2020, a political action committee aligned with Senate majority leader Chuck Schumer and Iowa Democratic Senate candidate Theresa Green-

As Senate minority leader in 2017, Democratic senator Chuck Schumer falsely promoted the idea that only the wealthiest Americans would benefit from the tax cut that President Trump proposed.

field pushed false information to undermine Greenfield's opponent, Senator Joni Ernst. In this case, an image of a fake email appeared on Facebook that purported that the Iowa Farm Bureau had rescinded its support for Ernst. In an agricultural state like Iowa, having the endorsement of the Farm Bureau affects the way many people vote. The Farm Bureau denied the validity of the claim and reaffirmed its endorsement of Ernst. Ernst went on to win the election. Nonetheless, the incident increased distrust among supporters of the two candidates. Indeed, spreading misinformation, disinformation, propaganda, and conspiracy theories has become a common way for political leaders, foreign nations, and extremist groups to create and amplify divisiveness. As Capitol police officer Michael Fanone, who was savagely beaten during the insurrection, points out, "Words have consequences."[27]

"Words have consequences."[27]

—Michael Fanone, US Capitol police officer

Combating Fake News

In 2020, researchers at the Stanford History Education Group, a research organization associated with Stanford University, released the results of a study to find out how well young people can distinguish between legitimate and fake news online. Over the course of ten months, a total of 3,446 middle school, high school, and college students in fourteen states completed a variety of assignments designed to measure their ability to evaluate online sources and information. One task, as an example, asked the students whether a website with articles about climate change was a reliable source of information. At first glance, the website appeared to be legitimate. But an online search indicated that it was associated with the fossil fuel industry, which has been known to deny established scientific facts about climate change for financial gains. Nevertheless, 96 percent of the subjects did not consider that ties to the fossil fuel industry might affect the reliability of the information on the website and rated the site as reliable.

In another assignment, the students were shown a video posted on Facebook that showed poll workers secretly cramming ballots into ballot boxes. Subtitles explained that the video was shot during the 2016 Democratic primary election. In reality, it was filmed during an election in Russia. Yet, rather than researching the roots of the video, most of the subjects accepted it as real. And, more than half agreed that the video provided strong evidence of voter fraud in the 2016 primary elections.

In reporting the results of the study, Sam Wineburg, the founder of the Stanford History Education Group, had this to say:

> If the results can be summarized in a single word, I would say they're troubling. . . . Many current high school students will be first-time voters. Our findings show that they are unprepared to assess the information they encounter. . . . By accepting these websites and videos at face value, students are making it too easy for bad actors to undermine faith in the democratic process. Thriving democracies need citizens who can evaluate and access reliable information.[28]

Social Media Platforms Take Action

Young people are not the only group tricked by unreliable online sources and information. People of all ages turn to social media platforms for news. Misinformation proliferates on these platforms. A 2019 Pew Research Center report found that about half of American adults who get their news online get news from Facebook, making it the most popular news source on social media. In comparison, 28 percent get news from YouTube, 17 percent from Twitter, and 14 percent from Instagram. And, like the students in the Stanford History Education Group study, these individuals, too, are often fooled by false posts. In fact, a 2019 joint study by researchers at Princeton and New York University found that people ages sixty-five and older were more likely to share misinformation they saw on Facebook than people in other age groups. Older Facebook users shared fake stories seven times more often than users who were eighteen to twenty-nine and twice as often as those ages forty-five to sixty-five.

Approximately 50 percent of American adults who get their news online rely on Facebook as their source for news reports.

Young or old, the more users share misinformation, the harder it is to contain. As misinformation is repeated, it becomes normalized and accepted as the truth. In an attempt to stop the viral spread of dangerous misinformation, social media sites have taken steps to remove fake news and fake accounts from their platforms. The vast amount of data and daily social media posts, however, makes it difficult to detect and stop fake news from circulating. About 500 million tweets, for example, are sent every day, and about 2 billion people use Facebook every month. Plus, according to a 2018 Massachusetts Institute of Technology study, false stories are seven times more likely to be retweeted than legitimate news.

Despite the huge challenge, social media platforms have been trying to identify, remove, and ban false information and its sources. However, quite a lot of fake news escapes detection. Using AI to collect and analyze massive quantities of data helps. By searching for key words and seemingly unconnected claims, AI can rapidly detect false posts, connections between posts, conspiracy theories, bot accounts, and deepfakes. In fact, by working with AI researchers at Michigan State University, Facebook developed new

AI technology that not only detects deepfakes but also identifies their origin. The technology is intended to help Facebook uncover coordinated efforts to spread these images before they go viral.

Facebook and other social media platforms also employ independent fact-checking organizations to help ferret out false information and images, fake groups, bots, and dangerous content that encourages violence. Once identified, the platforms remove these posts and the accounts where they originated. For instance, on January 7, 2021, Twitter, Facebook, and other mainstream social media platforms suspended Trump from their sites for spreading misinformation about voter fraud that encouraged the insurrection. In June 2021, Trump's Facebook suspension was evaluated by an independent oversight board set up by Facebook. This board, which began operation in 2020, handles appeals by Facebook users who believe their posts or accounts

Lawsuits Fighting Fake News

Disinformation is often created and spread to malign a specific person or to hurt a business's reputation and, therefore, its bottom line. Some businesses are fighting back by filing lawsuits against those spreading disinformation that defames their companies. Voting equipment companies, in particular, are in the forefront of these actions.

In March 2021, Dominion, a voting equipment company, filed a $1.6 million lawsuit against Fox News after broadcasters on the network aired the conspiracy theory that Dominion rigged its voting machines to change the results of the 2020 election. According to the lawsuit, "Fox sold a false story of election fraud in order to serve its own commercial purposes, severely injuring Dominion in the process."

The company also filed similar suits against individuals involved in spreading this conspiracy theory, as did an employee of the company who had received death threats based on this misinformation. The attorney who represents the above employee explains: "This goes beyond hoping to stop the disinformation. The goal that we have is to hold people accountable."

Quoted in Bente Birkeland, "Election Defamation Lawsuits Open New Front in Fight Against Disinformation," National Public Radio, March 27, 2021. www.npr.org.

have been wrongfully removed. In Trump's case, the board agreed that the suspension was justified, and it banned the president from Facebook and Instagram (which is owned by Facebook) for two years, at which time the ban will be reassessed.

Like Facebook, most mainstream social media platforms remove people and groups that spread fake news that threatens public safety and/or promotes hate speech and violence. As an example, Facebook banned Alex Jones from its platform, and Twitter removed about seventy thousand accounts associated with QAnon. Banning extremists' accounts, however, is not always effective. These groups just move to less mainstream, unregulated platforms, such as Parler, where they can continue to spread conspiracy theories and misinformation.

Political leaders are also being watched more closely. Some platforms, such as Twitter, prohibit all political ads. Likewise, Facebook ended its long-standing policy of shielding deceptive posts by politicians from being removed from the platform. Moreover, almost all platforms get rid of posts, accounts, and fake pages associated with bots and foreign governments. In 2019, Instagram removed fifty Russian-linked accounts in October alone.

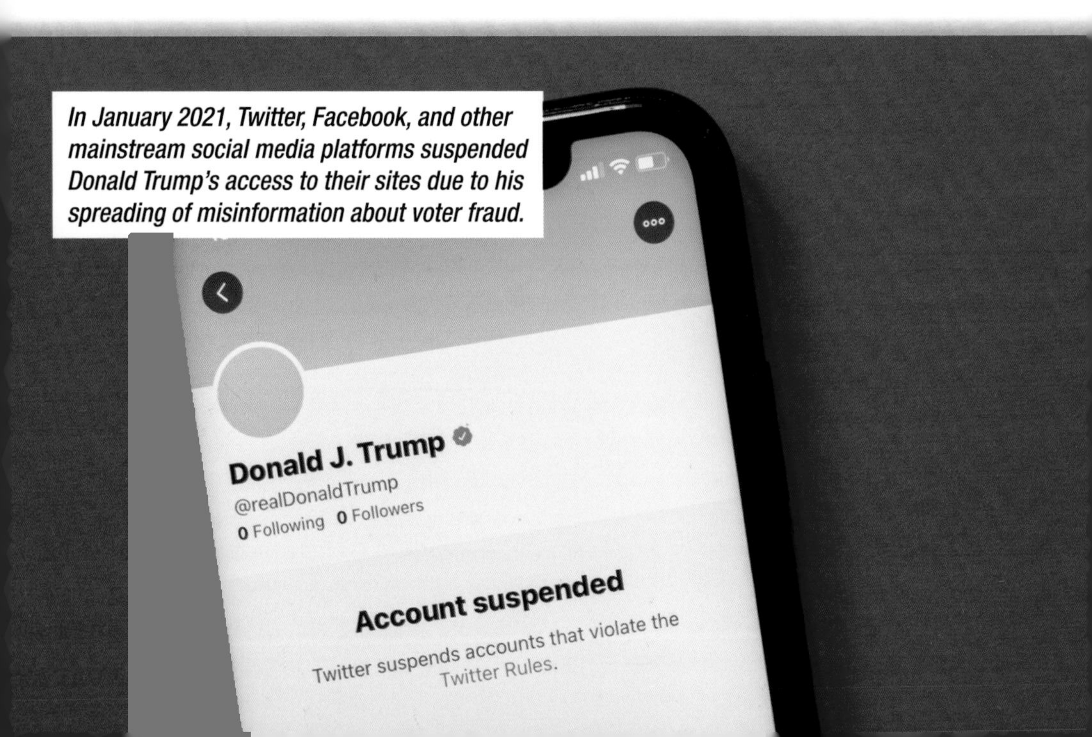

In January 2021, Twitter, Facebook, and other mainstream social media platforms suspended Donald Trump's access to their sites due to his spreading of misinformation about voter fraud.

When posts do not meet a platform's policies on removal but are, nonetheless, suspicious, some platforms have taken other steps to alert visitors to be cautious before sharing them. Twitter, as an example, puts blue checkmarks next to verified accounts. Facebook tried marking suspicious posts with a red flag icon. The company hoped the flag would keep visitors from engaging with the posts. However, the flags appeared to have the opposite effect. They seemed to entice visitors to read and share them. So, instead of the flags, Facebook added links to reputable related articles on pages with suspicious posts. Adding the links appears to have helped keep users from sharing questionable content.

Governmental Oversight vs. Free Speech

Despite these efforts, many Americans do not think that social media companies are doing enough or are acting quickly enough to protect society from fake news. Some of these individuals argue that the task is too large to leave in the hands of private businesses. Moreover, they worry that letting social media companies censor posts gives them too much power. They argue that media companies are, first and foremost, for-profit businesses, whose interests do not always coincide with those of the general public. These individuals want the government to step in and pass laws that make creating and spreading fake news through the media illegal. In an effort to reduce disinformation spread by foreign agents on social media, the House of Representatives passed the Foreign Agent Disclaimer Enhancement (FADE) Act in March 2021 as part of a larger bill known as the For the People Act. FADE requires that all politics-related social media posts made by any person or group representing the interests of a foreign government contain a disclaimer warning visitors of the post's origins and political content. If this disclaimer is not included, FADE requires that the Department of Justice make the platform remove the post.

As of July 2021, the act had not yet been brought before the US Senate for a vote. Supporters characterized it as a valuable tool for preserving democracy. According to Congresswoman Abigail Spanberger of Virginia, who cosponsored the bill,

> The United States must be on guard against those who seek to sow division and spread false information. Disclaimers on misleading, foreign-backed social media posts are often non-existent, particularly when content is shared or linked. In these instances, social media works as a rumor mill for disinformation. . . . By requiring foreign disclaimers within the actual content of social media posts, we can make sure the public knows the origins of information—and we can strengthen our democracy for the better.[29]

Other people disagree. They contend that policing by social media platforms and the government undermines the First Amendment of the US Constitution, which guarantees freedom of speech and freedom of the press, among other rights. In addition, many conservatives maintain that their views are more likely to be blocked than those of liberals. Indeed, after Facebook's independent advisory board upheld Trump's ban from the site, the former president sent out an email in which he suggested that the action was an attack on his right to free speech and his conservative views. "What Facebook, Twitter, and Google have done is a total disgrace and an embarrassment to our Country," he wrote, adding,

> Free Speech has been taken away from the President of the United States because the Radical Left Lunatics are afraid of the truth, but the truth will come out anyway, bigger and stronger than ever before. . . . The People of our Country will not stand for it! These corrupt social media companies must pay a political price, and must never again be allowed to destroy and decimate our Electoral Process.[30]

Those who oppose FADE argue that the right to freedom of speech gives people the right to express all kinds of information, including controversial and misleading ideas, and foreign propaganda. In their view, the proposed law would stifle harmless political speech, no matter the origin. The American Civil Liberties Union agrees. In its assessment, the bill would "unconstitutionally burden the speech and associational rights of many public interest organizations and American citizens. These provisions will chill speech essential to our public discourse and would do little to serve the public's legitimate interest."[31]

Many individuals are also concerned that passing such regulations gives the government too much power, which, in the wrong hands, could result in rampant censorship similar to that which

Reliable News Sites

It can be difficult to know whether or not a news site is trustworthy. However, there are several news sites that are generally considered reliable by multiple sources. Among these sources is *Forbes* magazine, which includes the following sites in its list:

Associated Press: The Associated Press is a news agency that provides news to print and broadcast news outlets.

British Broadcasting Corporation (BBC): The BBC provides unbiased world news on television and radio as well as online.

Cable News Network (CNN): CNN is a twenty-four-hour broadcast news channel, offering television and online news.

National Public Radio (NPR): NPR provides radio and online news and in-depth commentary.

New York Times: The *New York Times* has a liberal bias but provides factually correct print and online news.

Reuters: This media service is a good source of print and online breaking news.

Wall Street Journal: The *Wall Street Journal* has a conservative bias but provides factually correct print and online news.

Washington Post: The *Washington Post* has a liberal bias but provides factually correct print and online news.

occurs under authoritarian forms of government. As a 2019 report issued by the Library of Congress points out,

> While the dangers associated with the viral distribution of disinformation are widely recognized, the potential harm that may derive from disproportional measures to counter disinformation should not be underestimated. Unlimited governmental censorship of online communications; an expansive definition of what constitutes "disinformation"; broad application of emergency powers to block content based on grounds of national or public security; draconian penalties for alleged offenders without the ability to present an effective defense; and strict enforcement of defamation laws in the absence of journalistic defenses are just a few examples of potential threats to the principle of free speech and the administration of the rule of law posed by overreaching regulations concerning disinformation.[32]

Media Literacy Education

Clearly, whether or not social media platforms and/or the government should remove, regulate, or ban misinformation on social media is debatable. In fact, a 2021 Rasmussen national survey found that 49 percent of respondents were more concerned about the threat to free speech that imposing this type of censorship represents than about the threat fake news poses. Thirty-eight percent worried more about the threat of fake news, and 13 percent were undecided. Therefore, because it is so controversial, giving social media platforms and/or the government control of

"While the dangers associated with the viral distribution of disinformation are widely recognized, the potential harm that may derive from disproportional measures to counter disinformation should not be underestimated."[32]

—US Library of Congress

what can and cannot be posted may be unrealistic. That is why some organizations are helping to fill the gap by offering instruction in media literacy. Media literacy instruction teaches individuals to question whether what they are viewing online is supported by trusted sources and shows them how to search for evidence that verifies or debunks online claims. Such programs give people the tools they need to distinguish between fake and real news.

There are lots of these programs, with some targeting older people and many others focusing on teens. For example, one program, MediaWise's Teen Fact-Checking Network (TFCN), uses teens to fact-check trending stories and images and to teach viewers how to fact-check on their own. Using Instagram, YouTube, and other popular platforms, young fact-checkers post stories they have checked. Each story is accompanied by a step-by-step explanation of how the teen researched the story's credibility or lack of credibility. The aim is not only to discredit false information but also to help other teens gain the skills and confidence to fact-check on their own. The program appears to be working. In fact, 86 percent of respondents to an Instagram poll said that they were more likely to fact-check after viewing a TFCN post. As Katy Byron, the editor and program manager of MediaWise, explains, "If misinformation on the internet is a disease, then MediaWise is like the Red Cross."[33]

Everyone Can Help

Although all these efforts are steps in the right direction, the creators and spreaders of fake news are good at getting around roadblocks and making the misinformation they spread appear convincing. Media literacy instruction boosts people's ability to spot fake news. But even without the benefit of such instruction, there are steps individuals of all ages can take that will help control the spread of fake news.

The first step in determining whether an online, broadcast, or print story is factual or false is knowing what to look for. Although many false stories look and sound like legitimate news, there are certain features, such as sensational headlines and stories that play on the readers' emotions, that are common to fake news. As Alexa Volland, the head of the TFCN, explains, "If something online gives you an intense emotional reaction, that's a clue that it could be misinformation, if it makes you feel really angry or if it makes you feel validated. So instead of impulsively resharing, we really encourage teens and everyone to just hit the pause button and make sure that they have full context."[34]

Misspellings and incorrect grammar and punctuation are also tip-offs. Such posts are likely to be created by foreign agents. The information in the article is also a clue. Legitimate stories are usually backed by multiple reliable sources and multiple pieces of evidence; while fake news typically relies on a single source or piece of evidence. According to Volland, before accepting something as fact and sharing it with others, it is essential to determine "who was behind the information? What's the evidence? And what are other sources saying?"[35]

To help make these determinations, there are fact-checking websites that verify or debunk rumors, news articles, conspiracy theories, and other claims that appear on social media or other news sources. Some, such as the Pulitzer Prize–winning PolitiFact focus on claims made by elected officials. Others, such as SciCheck concentrate on scientific claims. Still others, such as Snopes, which is the largest fact-checking site on the internet, look into all sorts of stories and claims, including those related to science, health, politics, and technology. Snopes also provides accurate information from experts and trusted news sources to refute misinformation. And to help people know which news sources are reliable, Media Bias/Fact Check rates media outlets according to their biases.

It may seem time-consuming to check out information before circulating it, but the action is worth the effort, especially considering the threat that misinformation poses to society. When individuals, social media platforms, lawmakers, and others work together, progress can be made and the harm that misinformation causes can be inhibited.

SOURCE NOTES

Introduction: A Far-Reaching Problem

1. Quoted in Paul Blumenthal, "Capitol Insurrectionists Said They Were Following Trump's Orders," *Huffington Post*, January 16, 2021. www.huffpost.com.
2. Quoted in Sarah Al-Arshani, "The Department of Homeland Security Breaks from Trump and His Baseless Claims of Election Fraud, Calling This Year's Presidential Race 'the Most Secure in American History,'" Business Insider, November 13, 2020. www.businessinsider.com.
3. Timothy Garton Ash, "In the War of Fake News Versus Facts, Here's What the Next Battle Should Be," *The Guardian,* February 8, 2021. www.theguardian.com.

Chapter One: What Is Fake News?

4. Quoted in Josephine Harvey, "U.S. Olympic Athlete Sakura Kokumai Targeted in Racist Attack," *Huffington Post*, April 9, 2021. www.huffpost.com.
5. Sinan Aral, *The Hype Machine: How Social Media Disrupts Our Elections, Our Economy, and Our Health—and How We Must Adapt*. New York: Currency, 2020, p.26.
6. Andrew G. McCabe, *The Threat: How the FBI Protects America in the Age of Terror and Trump*. New York: St. Martin's, 2019.
7. Quoted in Thomas N. Edsall, "Democracy, Disrupted," *New York Times,* March 2, 2017. www.nytimes.com.
8. Quoted in Darrell M. West, "How to Combat Fake News and Disinformation," Brookings Institution, December 18, 2017. www.brookings.edu.
9. Quoted in Zara Abrams, "Controlling the Spread of Misinformation," American Psychological Association, March 1, 2021. www.apa.org.
10. Quoted in Jesse Singal, "Fake News Spreads Because People Trust Their Friends Too Much," Intelligencer, March 21, 2017. https://nymag.com.

11. Quoted in Tovia Smith, "'Exit Counselors' Strain to Pull Americans Out of a Web of False Conspiracies," National Public Radio, March 3, 2021. www.npr.org.

Chapter Two: Denying Science

12. Quoted in Timothy Johnson, "Alex Jones' Coronavirus Vaccine Conspiracy Theories Are a Public Health Threat," Media Matters, December 14, 2020. www.mediamatters.org.
13. Quoted in Marianna Spring and Mike Wendling, "How Covid-19 Myths Are Merging with the QAnon Conspiracy Theory," *BBC Trending* (blog), British Broadcasting Corporation, September 3, 2020. www.bbc.com.
14. Quoted in Zack Budryk, "Conspiracy Theorists Who Claim 5G Linked to Coronavirus Believed to Burn Cell Towers in Europe," *The Hill,* April 21, 2020. https://thehill.com.
15. Quoted in United Nations, "During This Coronavirus Pandemic, 'Fake News' Is Putting Lives at Risk: UNESCO," UN News, April 2020. https://news.un.org.
16. Quoted in David Gorski, "Scientists and Physicians Versus the Central Conspiracy Theory of Science Denial," *Respectful Insolence* (blog), December 9, 2020. https://respectfulinsolence.com.
17. Quoted in Jay Reeves, "Rise in Virus Cases Worries US Surgeon General," *Albuquerque Journal,* July 19, 2021, p. A6.
18. Quoted in Elizabeth Weise, "How Does COVID-19 End in the US? Likely with a Death Rate Americans Are Willing to 'Accept,'" *USA Today,* June 6, 2021. www.msn.com.

Chapter Three: Stoking Divisiveness

19. Quoted in Jeff Seldin, "US Accuses Foreign, Online Actors of Inflaming Tensions," Voice of America, June 4, 2020. www.voanews.com.
20. Quoted in Mary Papenfuss, "1,000 Paid Russian Trolls Spread Fake News on Hillary Clinton, Senate Intelligence Heads Told," *Huffington Post,* March 31, 2017. www.huffpost.com.
21. Quoted in Veronica Stracqualursi, "*Washington Post* Corrects Report That Giuliani Was Warned He Was Target of Russian Influence Campaign," CNN, May 1, 2021. https://edition.cnn.com.
22. Quoted in Kevin Breuninger, "Russia and Iran Tried to Interfere with 2020 Election, U.S. Intelligence Agencies Say," MSN News, March 16, 2021. www.msn.com.
23. Quoted in Elizabeth Dwoskin and Craig Timberg, "The Unseen Machine Pushing Trump's Social Media Megaphone into Overdrive," *Washington Post,* October 30, 2020. www.msn.com.

24. Quoted in Ben Sales, "White Supremacist Arrested for Threatening to Kill Democrats, Federal Officials," *Pittsburgh Jewish Chronicle*, November 11, 2020. https://jewishchronicle.timesofisrael.com.
25. Philip Bump, "It's Not Just Going to Go Away," *Washington Post*, May 4, 2021. www.washingtonpost.com.
26. Quoted in Katie Riga, "Republicans at Jan. 6 Hearing Try to Paint Trump and His Followers as the True Victims," Talking Points Memo, May 12, 2021. https://talkingpointsmemo.com.
27. Quoted in Stephen Collinson, "The Republican Party's Mission: Whitewash the Trump Presidency," CNN, June 18, 2021. www.cnn .com.

Chapter Four: Combating Fake News

28. Quoted in Carrie Spector, "High School Students Are Unprepared to Judge the Credibility of Information on the Internet, According to Stanford Researchers," Stanford News, November 18, 2019. https://news.stanford.edu.
29. Quoted in Maggie Miller, "House Lawmakers Reintroduce Bipartisan Bill to Weed Out Foreign Disinformation on Social Media," *The Hill,* January 22, 2021. https://thehill.com.
30. Quoted in Joe Dwinell, "Trump Blasts Facebook for Extending Ban, Calls It a Crime Against Free Speech," *Boston Herald,* May 5, 2021. www.bostonherald.com.
31. Quoted in Liz George, "House Passes Bill Allowing DOJ to Force Deletion of Social Media Posts from Select Users," American Military News, March 5, 2021. https://americanmilitarynews.com.
32. Ruth Levush, "Government Responses to Disinformation on Social Media Platforms: Comparative Summary," Library of Congress, January 30, 2020. www.loc.gov.
33. Quoted in Adam Chiara, "Let's Teach 1 Million Teenagers How to Spot Fake News by 2020," *The Hill,* January 9, 2019. https://thehill .com.
34. Quoted in Robin Young and Allison Hagan, "'Everything's Worth a Fact-Check': Network Teaches Teens to Debunk Online Myths," *Here & Now,* WBUR, August 11, 2020. www.wbur.org.
35. Quoted in Young and Hagan, "'Everything's Worth a Fact-Check.'"

HOW TO SPOT FAKE NEWS

Here are some tips from the International Federation of Library Associations and Institutions to help people spot fake news.

Consider the Source
Click away from the story to investigate the site, its mission, and its contact info.

Read Beyond
Headlines can be outrageous in an effort to get clicks. What is the whole story?

Check the Author
Do a quick search on the author. Is the author credible? Is the author real?

Supporting Sources?
Click on those links. Determine whether the info given actually supports the story.

Check the Date
Reposting old news stories does not mean they are relevant to current events.

Is It a Joke?
If it is too outlandish, it might be satire. Research the site and author to be sure.

Check Your Biases
Consider if your own beliefs could affect your judgment.

Ask the Experts
Ask a librarian, or consult a fact-checking website.

International Federation of Library Associations and Institutions, "Fake News, Propaganda, and Disinformation: Learning to Critically Evaluate Media Sources: Infographic: Spot Fake News," Cornell University Library, July 14, 2021. https://guides.library.cornell.edu/evaluate_news/infographic.

American Enterprise Institute (AEI)
www.aei.org

The AEI is a conservative-leaning think tank. It provides articles, reports, posts, speeches, and podcasts concerning free speech and other issues associated with fake news and misinformation.

Austin Community College (ACC) Library Services
https://library.austincc.edu

This online library offers ebooks, journals, reference materials, videos, and research guides on all sorts of topics, including a research guide with articles, studies, and statistics related to fake news.

Brookings Institution
www.brookings.edu

The Brookings Institution is a public policy organization that conducts research and provides information, reports, articles, and policy recommendations about issues facing society, including information on recognizing and combating disinformation.

GCF Global
https://edu.gcfglobal.org/en/digital-media-literacy

GCF Global is a free online learning site. It includes the GCF-LearnFree.org program, which offers tutorials, lessons, videos, and information on many topics, including a large section on digital media literacy.

Harvard Kennedy School Misinformation Review
https://misinforeview.hks.harvard.edu

This website from Harvard University offers lots of articles about disinformation, propaganda, conspiracy theories, information bias, fake news, media literacy, public policy related to fake news, and much more.

National Public Radio (NPR)
www.npr.org

NPR provides articles, reports, interviews, and stories on a wide range of topics on its website. Among these is a special series of articles on the fake news crisis under the heading "Untangling Disinformation." There are also many articles dealing with misinformation related to the COVID-19 pandemic.

PolitiFact
www.politifact.org

PolitiFact is a non-partisan fact-checking organization that focuses on political news. It rates statements made by politicians for accuracy. It also partners with Facebook and TikTok to try to slow the spread of disinformation on these platforms.

Poynter Institute for Media Studies
www.poynter.org

The Poynter Institute is a world leader in improving journalism to strengthen democracy. It specializes in training journalists, providing media literacy education, fact-checking, and news reporting. It houses the political fact-checking sites PolitiFact, MediaWise, and the TFCN.

Snopes
www.snopes.com

Snopes is a large, well-respected fact-checking and investigative reporting website. It links to and documents its sources so that readers can do further research and come to their own conclusions.

FOR FURTHER RESEARCH

Books

John Allen, *How Does Fake News Threaten Society?* San Diego: ReferencePoint, 2021.

Kari Cornell, *Fake News.* San Diego: BrightPoint, 2020.

Michael Miller, *Fake News: Separating Truth from Fiction.* Minneapolis: Twenty-First Century, 2019.

Carla Mooney, *Fake News and the Manipulation of Public Opinion.* San Diego: ReferencePoint, 2019.

Cindy L. Otis, *True or False: A CIA Analyst's Guide to Spotting Fake News*. New York: Feiwel and Friends, 2020.

Internet Sources

Corby Brooke, "Misinformation Spreads like Wildfire," *The Guilfordian*, April 14, 2021. www.guilfordian.com.

Alia E. Dastagir, "Anyone Can Fall for 'Fake News,' Conspiracy Theories: The Psychology of Misinformation," *USA Today,* January 20, 2021. www.usatoday.com.

Milos Djordjevic, "27 Alarming Fake News Statistics on the Effects of False Reporting (the 2021 Edition)," Letter.ly, April 1, 2021. https://letter.ly.

Filippo Menczer and Thomas Hills, "Information Overload Helps Fake News Spread, and Social Media Knows It," *Scientific American,* December 1, 2020. www.scientificamerican.com.